THE
100+
SERIES™

Reproducible Activities

M000086754

Daily Warmups

Math Problems & Puzzles

Grade 6

Instructional Fair
An imprint of Carson-Dellosa Publishing LLC
Greensboro, North Carolina®

Instructional Fair
An imprint of Carson-Dellosa Publishing LLC
P.O. Box 35665
Greensboro, NC 27425 USA

Printed in the USA • All rights reserved.   ISBN: 0-7424-1796-4

5 6 7 8 9 10 11 GLO 15 14 13 12 11 10   10510019763

Table of Contents

NCTM Standard	Problem Number
Number and Operations	4, 8, 11, 15, 22, 25, 29, 33, 42, 46, 53, 58, 64, 68, 79, 83, 88, 92, 98, 106, 112, 121, 132, 140, 146, 149, 157, 164, 171, 175, 178, 184, 187, 190, 196, 202, 204, 207, 211, 215, 221, 223, 226, 229, 233
Algebra	3, 9, 16, 20, 26, 34, 44, 51, 60, 66, 73, 80, 100, 108, 115, 125, 131, 138, 151, 161, 170, 179, 189, 195, 203, 232
Geometry	5, 10, 17, 24, 28, 32, 39, 48, 54, 62, 69, 76, 86, 96, 105, 114, 120, 129, 137, 145, 154, 163, 169, 174, 181, 191, 199, 205, 212, 217, 228
Measurement	2, 7, 13, 36, 55, 61, 71, 78, 89, 95, 99, 104, 113, 122, 130, 136, 141, 148, 153, 159, 165, 172, 185, 192, 198, 210, 218, 231
Probability and Statistics	6, 18, 27, 38, 45, 52, 63, 72, 81, 93, 102, 111, 119, 124, 133, 143, 158, 168, 177, 186, 193, 200, 214, 220
Problem Solving	21, 31, 35, 43, 50, 59, 70, 77, 87, 94, 101, 109, 116, 123, 128, 142, 150, 155, 160, 166, 176, 183, 188, 194, 201, 209, 219, 225, 234
Logical Reasoning	1, 14, 23, 37, 41, 49, 56, 65, 74, 82, 90, 97, 107, 118, 127, 134, 147, 152, 162, 167, 182, 188, 208, 216, 222, 227
Patterns and Functions	12, 19, 29, 40, 47, 57, 67, 75, 84, 91, 103, 110, 117, 126, 135, 139, 144, 156, 173, 197, 206, 213, 224

Introduction

This book is one in a series of books from grade K through grade 8. Each book provides a wide variety of challenging and engaging grade-appropriate problems and puzzles from all areas of the math curriculum. Each book contains 234 problems and puzzles, one for each day of the school year plus more. All are keyed to the appropriate NCTM standards, and many are designed for hands-on problem solving with common classroom manipulatives. Several problems call for the use of tangrams. For your convenience, we have included a reproducible set on page 5. Other problems call for protractors, dice, centimeter cubes, geoboards, pentominoes, and calculators. However, most problems require only paper and pencil and a little brainpower.

Each page contains two problems or puzzles. The problems are reproducible and are suitable for overhead use. Most offer ample space for problem solving. The problems and puzzles in this book are designed to be solved within 15 minutes, but most will take 5 minutes or less. These problems are great for use as early morning warm-ups or for the beginning of math class and can be worked independently or in groups. You can also assign problems as homework or as a math lab activity. Another idea is to use these problems in contests. Which group or individual will be the first to solve the problem?

Work through a few problems before your students begin to work independently or in groups. As you do so, it's important to model a problem-solving process. Stress that many problems have multiple solutions. Then, watch as your students grow and develop their own problem-solving strategies and gain a new appreciation for math.

Tangrams

1 Logical Reasoning

Aaron has three brothers: Brendan, Cole, and Devin. Use the clues to calculate the age of each boy.

Clue 1 Brendan is twice as old as Cole.

Clue 2 The sum of Aaron and Devin's ages equals Brendan's age.

Clue 3 The sum of Cole and Devin's ages equals Aaron's age.

Clue 4 The sum of all four boys' ages is forty.

2 Measurement

On Saturday, Simon the baker decides to make a large batch of chocolate-chip cookies. His basic recipe calls for 24 ounces of chocolate chips, but he decides to make five times that amount. How many pounds of chocolate chips will Simon need?

0-7424-1796-4 *Daily Warmups*

Algebra

3

Draw a Venn diagram to show the relationship between
A) all numbers, B) odd numbers, C) multiples of 5, and D) factors of 60.
Label each part of your diagram.

Number and Operations

4

Begin with 1,234,567. Increase the number in the tens place by 2.
Decrease the ten-thousands place by 1. Switch the digit in the ones
place with the digit in the hundred-thousands place. Add 5 million.
What is your final number?

0-7424-1796-4 *Daily Warmups*

Geometry

A very famous, but absent-minded, professor visited math class today and lost his favorite geometry model. It is a rectangle with two congruent parts. Because he is absent minded, he can't even remember what the congruent parts look like. He does remember the rectangle. Help the professor out by drawing two rectangles. Then divide each into congruent parts.

Statistics

Find the range, mean, median, and mode of these numbers:

18, 14, 90, 27, 18, 1, 85, 13

Measurement

The Parents' Club decided to put additional play surface on the school grounds. It was designed to be a 50-foot square. But the science club needed one-half of the area for a native plant garden. The playing surface was cut in half diagonally. What is the perimeter and area of the new play surface?

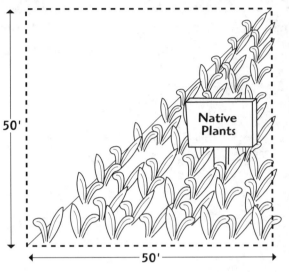

Number and Operations

You can make 50¢ using many different coin combinations. List the coin combinations to answer the questions below.

a How can you make 50¢ using exactly 46 coins?

b How can you make 50¢ using exactly 22 coins?

c How can you make 50¢ using exactly 7 coins?

Algebra

Teacher Connie Cash worked as a cashier at the Kid's Carnival. She was amazed at the number of students who couldn't count change! So on Monday she assigned this problem to her class: You need to make change for $0.50. Write an algebraic equation that models this problem. Then list as many possible solutions as you can.

Geometry

Use graph paper or make a rough sketch of a graph. Number the horizontal axis from 1 to 11. Number the vertical axis from 0 to 4 or more. Connect the points in the order drawn, and connect the last point with the first point. What shape have you made?

(6, 4) (4, 1) (9, 1) (11, 4)

Number and Operations

Which set of numbers has the largest greatest common factor?

 a 42, 56, 84

 b 34, 72, 98

 c 21, 63, 91

Patterns and Functions

Kyle is training for the Waterfront 6K Race. He will run a total of 60 blocks during this training run. Kyle likes to pace himself during training, changing his speed every five blocks. He begins by running the first five blocks in 15 minutes. He runs the second five blocks in 10 fewer seconds than the first five. He runs the third five blocks in 10 fewer seconds than the second five. If he continues to increase his speed in this way, how long will it take him to run the 60th block?

Measurement

The Pep Band has decided to decorate the gymnasium for the Girls State Basketball Championship. The gym is 60 yards long and 30 yards wide. How many feet of crepe paper will they need to create a red, a white, a blue, and a yellow stripe all the way around the gym? How much will each color of crepe paper cost if a five-yard package costs $2.17?

Logical Reasoning

Rachel has two younger sisters. One is 2 years old and the other is 10 years old. The combined age of the three girls is 22. How can that be true?

Number and Operations

Which of the following numbers are divisible by 9? Carlos looked at the numbers and instantly knew. What was his secret?

a 346   **b** 5,211   **c** 8,013   **d** 12,672   **e** 9,091,287

Algebra

Use a calculator.

Mr. Clark uses a function machine to generate problems for math homework. He programs a rule and then the machine uses it to change the numbers for each problem. Take a look at the numbers in the table. See if you can name the rule. Use the rule to complete the table.

Number in	Number out
12	144
25	625
30	900
10	—
11	—
13	—
18	—
32	—

Geometry

Alex is preparing a new garden plot. His original plot was 13 feet by 20 feet, but he plans to double the length of each side. How many yards of fencing are required for a rectangular plot that measures 26 feet by 40 feet? By how much is Alex increasing the area of his garden?

Probability

Use real or play coins to answer these questions.

a What are the odds that flipping a coin will result in heads?

b What are the odds that two sixth graders, each flipping a coin, will both get heads?

c What are the odds that three sixth graders, each flipping a coin, will all get heads?

d Have four friends each flip a coin with you. What do you think are the odds that all four of you will get heads?

Patterns and Functions

19

Mac's Door-to-Door Delivery has been having a terrible time with the doors on their largest truck. They started the morning with a full load of 3,000 pounds. Each time they went over a bump, they lost 25% of the load that was still on the truck. Make a "bump" line to chart the diminishing weight in the back of the truck. Round all of your figures to the nearest tenth.

Algebra

20

Caitlin and eight of her cousins decided they wanted to keep in better touch. Once a week, they will each e-mail everyone else in the group. How many e-mails will be sent each week?

Problem Solving

How many combinations of coins totaling 50¢ can be made without using pennies?

Number and Operations

Alice is writing a sports article for the school newsletter. She wants to compare the girls' basketball team's win-loss ratio to the boys' basketball team's win-loss ratio. The boys' team has won 12 of their 16 games. The girls' team has won 14 of their 16 games. Find the win-loss ratio for each team.

Logical Reasoning

Justin asked his grandfather how old he was. The man replied, "I started school when I was five years old. I spent the next ten years at the same school. Then I went to high school for four years, and one year later, I joined the Army. I spent exactly 50% of my age today in the Army and retired 25 years ago."

How old is Justin's grandfather today?

Geometry

Mr. Van Goe is in charge of designing a mural for the front of the middle school. The local art store donated polygon-shaped materials, but there aren't enough to go around for all the sixth graders. Mr. Van Goe needs your help creating more sides using the existing shapes. Find a way to increase the number of sides in each polygon below. Draw a line segment to divide each shape into two new shapes. Then write how many sides the two new polygons have altogether.

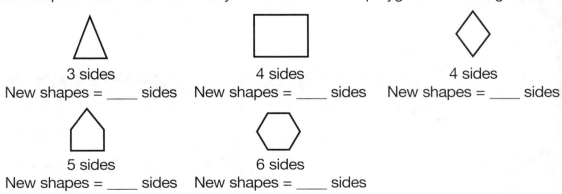

3 sides
New shapes = ____ sides

4 sides
New shapes = ____ sides

4 sides
New shapes = ____ sides

5 sides
New shapes = ____ sides

6 sides
New shapes = ____ sides

Number and Operations

Complete the pattern for each row. If the pattern continues in the same way, what will be the tenth rational number?

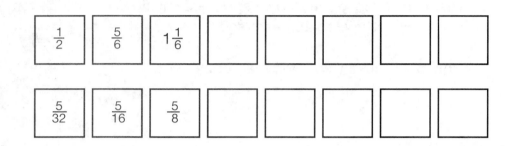

$\frac{1}{2}$	$\frac{5}{6}$	$1\frac{1}{6}$					

$\frac{5}{32}$	$\frac{5}{16}$	$\frac{5}{8}$					

Algebra

The students at Kennedy School held a car wash to raise money for new software in the library. They charged $5.00 for each car. The first hour they washed 5 cars. The next hour they washed 7 cars. The third hour they washed 9 cars. Every hour they washed 2 more cars than the hour before. At this rate, how many cars did they wash altogether in 8 hours? How much money did they earn?

Probability

Use centimeter cubes and a plastic bag.

You have been asked to watch all 20 of Ms. Loveland's kindergarten students on the playground. Before you can stop them, every one of them has thrown both shoes down the storm drain where you can't see them. Using a stick, you pull the shoes out one at a time. What are the odds that the second shoe you pull up will match the first? Predict. Then test your prediction by putting cubes in the bag and drawing them out one at a time. Record your results.

Geometry

Glimdorf does not understand Earth time. When someone asked him what time it was he replied, "180 degrees." What time was it?

Patterns and Functions

Find the pattern in each row of numbers.

a 8, 16, 32, 64, 128, 256, ____, ____

b 23, 25, 28, 30, 33, 35, ____, ____

c 30, 38, 47, 57, 68, 80, ____, ____

Number and Operations

Use one of these fractions in each space to make a true equation.

$$\frac{3}{4}, \quad \frac{1}{4}, \quad \frac{1}{3}, \quad \frac{1}{2}, \quad \frac{5}{6}, \quad \frac{1}{12}$$

a $\frac{1}{6}$ + ____ + ____ = 1

b ____ + ____ − $\frac{5}{12}$ = $\frac{7}{12}$

c $\frac{5}{6}$ + ____ + ____ = $1\frac{5}{12}$

d $\frac{1}{12}$ + ____ − ____ = $\frac{5}{12}$

e ____ + $\frac{7}{12}$ + ____ = $1\frac{1}{6}$ = $1\frac{5}{6}$

Problem Solving

At one time, 30,000 Americans held reservations on Pan American Airline's first flights to the moon. If the space shuttle—the only way now to fly close to the moon—can seat only eight passengers comfortably, estimate the number of trips Pan Am would have to make to serve all of the customers with reservations for flights to the moon—if Pan Am owned a shuttle and if they had not gone out of business.

Geometry

Count the number of right triangles in this figure.

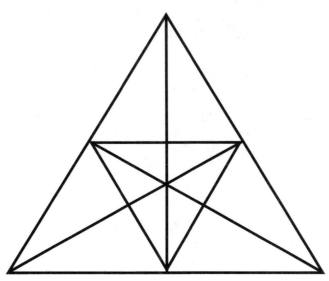

Number and Operations

Use a calculator.

Use a different number to fill in each space in the puzzle.
The sum of the numbers in each row and column is 3.5.

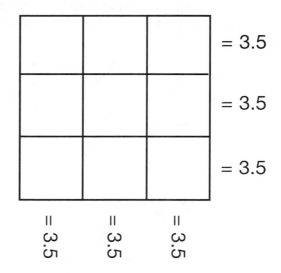

= 3.5

= 3.5

= 3.5

= 3.5   = 3.5   = 3.5

Algebra

Peter and Jessica are working at the Snack Shack selling hot dogs at the softball tournament. In the first hour, Peter sells 14 hot dogs and Jessica sells 20. In the second hour, Peter sells 20 and Jessica sells 25. In the third hour, Peter sells 26 and Jessica sells 30. If they continue selling hot dogs at the same rate, during what hour will they sell the same number of hot dogs?

Problem Solving

Find the total number of cubes in each of the figures below.

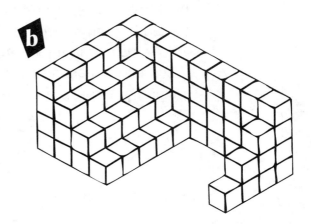

Measurement

Justin, Aaron's younger brother, has decided to measure everything he does in seconds. If he is in school for 7 hours and 32 minutes, how many seconds is he there? Do you think that measuring everything in seconds will make time seem to move more quickly or more slowly for Justin?

Logical Reasoning

Heather is helping out at Sunshine Preschool. At noon, she noticed that $\frac{1}{2}$ of the children were missing. When she called for them, $\frac{1}{2}$ of the missing children returned to the room. But as soon as Heather turned her back, $\frac{1}{2}$ of the children in the room left again. Of those who remained in the room, $\frac{1}{2}$ played with blocks, $\frac{1}{3}$ played with the dress-up clothes, and the rest looked at books. If just one child is looking at a book, how many children were in the room before noon?

Probability

Use two regular dice.

Joab and Kai are playing a game with dice. They roll both dice and then subtract the smaller number from the larger number. Joab gets 10 points for each answer that is an odd number, and Kai gets 10 points for each answer that is an even number. Is the game fair? Why, or why not? If it is not fair, how would you change the rules?

Geometry

For Math, Greta had to write five statements about polygons.
Read over the statements. Circle any statements that are impossible.

a A quadrilateral can have 2 pairs of parallel lines and 2 pairs of sides that are equal.

b A straight line that connects two vertices of a polygon is called a diagonal.

c A rhombus is a parallelogram.

d A trapezoid has 2 pairs of parallel lines.

e A rhombus has 4 congruent sides.

Logical Reasoning

Sook was about to throw away her collection of Mega-Mutant Hero cards when she saw this ad in the paper:

Wanted
Old trading cards. Will pay top dollar.
Five-year-old cards: $1.00 each
Six-year-old cards: $1.50 each
Seven-year-old cards: $2.25 each
Eight-year-old cards: $3.25 each

If this pattern continued, how much would a 12-year-old Mega-Mutant card be worth?

Logical Reasoning

There are five children in the Gonzalez family. The youngest is in third grade. The oldest is twice as old as the youngest. The triplets are four years younger than the oldest. The product of all the children's ages is 221,184. How old is each child?

Number and Operations

Use a calculator.

Kara, the student body treasurer, bought some snacks for the student council meeting. She used some coupons to save money, but the receipt was ripped somehow and she lost half of it. Now she's confused about how to report what she spent. Take a look at the receipt. Find which amounts are for purchases (+) and which are for coupon refunds (–). Write the number sentence Kara can use at the student council meeting.

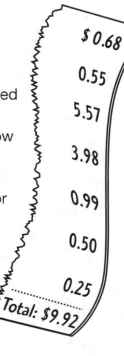

$ 0.68
0.55
5.57
3.98
0.99
0.50
0.25
Total: $9.92

Problem Solving

Eileen wants to share a pie with 13 of her friends. She is determined to give everyone a serving, despite the size of the serving. Help Eileen cut the pie into 14 slices using only five straight cuts.

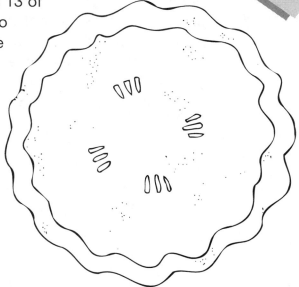

Algebra

Mason is stocking the Snack Shack with sports beverages. He puts out twice as many bottles of tropical punch as lemon-lime, 10 more bottles of lemon-lime than fruit punch, four times as many bottles of fruit punch as orange, two fewer bottles of orange than grape, and 9 bottles of grape. How many bottles of sports beverage does Mason put in the Snack Shack?

Probability

Some things are more predictable than others. Which of the following can you not easily determine the probability of?

a That you will accidentally trip while walking to your next class.

b That when rolling two dice, two numbers that can add up to six appear face up.

c That you will climb Mount Everest after school.

d That at least one baby born within the next hour will be named Agnes.

Number and Operations

Find the mystery number.

I'm a three-digit palindrome.

The product of my digits is divisible by 5.

What number am I?

Patterns and Functions

Complete these pattern analogies.

5 is to 25 as 6 is to ____

$\frac{1}{4}$ is to $\frac{1}{2}$ as 0.25 is to ____

$\frac{1}{5}$ is to $\frac{4}{5}$ as 0.2 is to ____

7 is to 77 as 11 is to ____

Geometry

Circle the shapes that are not regular polygons.

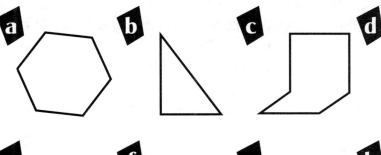

Logical Reasoning

Use 24 toothpicks to make 8 squares of equal size. Draw your solution below.

Problem Solving

John agreed to take over his brother's paper route while his brother was out of town. John's mother drove while John threw the papers. Out of a total route of 320 papers, John missed four times the number of front door areas as he hit. How many papers landed at the front door?

Algebra

The Ladies' Auxiliary Group donated $1,500.00 to the middle school to support three student groups: the choir, the band, and the student council. The band spent twice as much as the choir. The student council spent three times as much as the choir. How much did each group spend?

Probability

Hillside Mall is holding its annual Marvelous May Contest. Twenty-five people, including Allison, have won the chance to reach inside the Pirate's Chest and pull out the key to the mall, which entitles the bearer to a $1,000 shopping spree. There are 13 other keys in the chest along with 860 key-shaped pretzels, 500 plastic key rings, and 600 five-dollar gift certificates folded into small metal tubes. What are the odds that Allison will reach in and pull out the winning key? Given the number of prizes in the Pirate's Chest, is there a statistical advantage in going first rather than twenty-fifth?

Number and Operations

Jesse went to Cone Zone and wanted to order a three-scoop ice cream cone. He chose one scoop each of Screaming Strawberry, Freaky Fudge, and Very Vanilla. How many different ways could the scoops be arranged on the cone?

Geometry

Name the polygon below. Then draw a diagonal from the vertex marked X to the nonadjacent vertices. Name the shapes made by the diagonals.

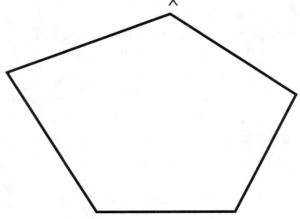

Measurement

Use a geoboard and rubber bands.

Make five different shapes that have a perimeter 12-units long. Draw the shapes. Do your shapes have the same area?

Logical Reasoning

Stephen, his sister Meagan, Carlos, and Alexa are playing a game at Carlos's kitchen table. Use these clues and a diagram to decide where each person is sitting. Everyone sits facing the table.

- Stephen is not sitting next to his sister.
- Carlos is sitting to the right of Meagan's brother's partner.

Patterns and Functions

Jordan has developed a combination radio, CD player, television, cellular phone, and game player that fits in the palm of his hand. Unfortunately, the batteries needed to power his invention are huge and don't last long. When the batteries are new, they last four hours before they need to be recharged. After the first charge, they last only 3.8 hours. After the second charge, they last just 3.4 hours, and after the third charge just 2.8 hours. What will eventually happen to the batteries? When will that happen?

Number and Operations

Angella and four of her friends spend the weekend painting the Recreation Room at Clark Retirement Home. Each of them painted a fraction of the room. Who painted the largest area? Put the painters in order from largest to smallest.

Angella: $\frac{2}{7}$ Ramon: $\frac{2}{12}$ Timothy: $\frac{2}{9}$ Grace: $\frac{1}{5}$ Justin: $\frac{1}{8}$

Problem Solving

59

The hit movie this fall is "My Sister Is from Saturn." If the theater that features the movie opens at 10:00 A.M. and closes at 10:00 P.M., and the cleanup crew needs 30 minutes after each showing to clean the theater, how many times can the 105-minute movie be shown in a day?

Algebra

60

Find the mystery number.

I am less than 150 and greater than 100.

I am divisible by 7 and by 5.

What am I?

Measurement

Use one set of tangram pieces.

Assume that the small triangle has two units of area. Create shapes that have 6 units of area, 8 units of area, and 12 units of area. Trace the shapes and label them with the units of area.

Geometry

Kevin is working on an art project. He wants to make a pattern for an open box that will always have a star on the bottom. Which one of these designs will work?

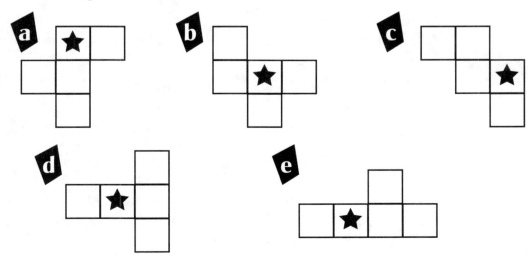

Probability

Mr. Weisenheimer is teaching his students about probability. He pulls four cards from a bag. On each of the cards a number is written:

| 4 | 6 | 0 | 1 |

How many different four-digit numbers can be formed from the four numbers using each numeral only once?

Number and Operations

Circle the seven prime numbers that, when added together, equal 98.

3, 11, 14, 13, 5, 17, 12, 6, 19, 23, 7, 9

0-7424-1796-4 *Daily Warmups*

Logical Reasoning

Esther is doing a survey to see how many people have sisters and how many have brothers. Out of the 26 people she has surveyed, 18 have sisters, 14 have brothers, and 6 have both brothers and sisters. How many people have only sisters and how many have only brothers? If desired, use a Venn diagram to solve this problem.

Algebra

Mr. Jones formed three problem-solving teams in his class. Each team was asked to bring three colored markers, four times the number of rulers as markers, and twice the number of sheets of graph paper as rulers. How many sheets of paper did the class bring altogether?

Patterns and Functions

The town of Pine Grove has a dog-at-large problem. Last week, the town council passed a tough new law. The first time a dog is picked up running at large, the owner must pay a $25.00 fine and spend two hours cleaning the town's parks. Each repeat offense carries a $5.00 increase in the fine and an additional one-half hour cleaning the parks. If Kerry must now spend six hours cleaning, how many times has his dog been caught without a leash, and how much is the current fine?

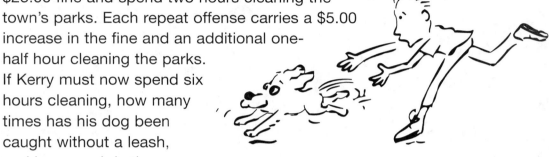

Number and Operations

Brittany and Alonzo collected this number of cans during the week:

Monday: A prime number that is < 20 and > 17.

Tuesday: A number that is the square of 4.

Wednesday: A number that is the greatest common factor (GCF) of 20 and 40.

Thursday: The GCF of 54 and 60.

Friday: A prime number > 62 and < 70.

On which day did they collect the greatest number of cans? On which day did they collect the fewest number of cans? How many cans did they collect altogether?

Geometry

Mrs. Majesky's class invented a new game that involves football, soccer, and water balloons. The playing field is 180 yards long but only 5 feet wide. What is the total area of this playing field?

Problem Solving

Six percent of the gasoline used by automobiles in the United States is burned while the cars are idling in traffic jams. If the average car uses 480 gallons of gasoline a year, how many gallons does it burn in traffic jams? If the average price of a gallon of gas in 2001 was $1.40, how much money did the average car waste on gas burned in traffic jams?

Measurement

Consider these two facts:

- A human being breathes approximately six quarts of air every minute.
- There are about 14,625,000 people living in New York City.

How many gallons of air do New Yorkers consume in just one minute?

Statistics

The following table shows the number of rebounds Melodie had during her last basketball season. What are the median, mode, and average number of rebounds she had for the season?

Game	1	2	3	4	5	6	7	8	9	10	11	12	13	14
Rebounds	8	7	6	9	4	7	9	8	10	12	6	4	18	6

Median:

Mode:

Average:

Algebra

What are all the numbers that could be written in ⬡ to make true sentences?

$$\bigcirc - 6 \leq 7$$

Logical Reasoning

Jamilla is walking through the forest with her rabbit, cat, and bird. Suddenly she comes to a river. A tiny rubber boat sits by the riverbank. The boat can hold only two of them. Jamilla can't leave the cat alone with the rabbit, and she can't leave the cat alone with the bird. How many trips must Jamilla make across the river before she and all her pets are safely to the other side?

Use a diagram to help you solve this problem.

Patterns and Functions

Sophie's brother collects baseball cards. Last week be bought some cards and paid $8.00 for every six cards he bought. Yesterday he sold them and made a profit of $4.00 on every three cards. If he made a profit of $24.00 altogether, how many cards did he buy and then sell?

Geometry

Use two sets of tangrams.

Can you make each of these shapes? In the table, list the number of tangram pieces you used.

Shape	Number of Sides	Number of Pieces Used to Make the Polygon
a. triangle		
b. square		
c. pentagon		
d. hexagon		
e. heptagon		
f. octagon		

Problem Solving

The science class built model rockets. Jack's rocket reached an altitude of 375 feet. Clarissa and Skylar's model reached an altitude 160% that of Jack's. T.J. and Camilla built a larger rocket which reached an altitude only $\frac{4}{5}$ that of Clarissa and Skylar's. List the altitude each team's rocket reached.

Measurement

The moon is 238,900 miles from the earth. The Sears Tower in Chicago is 1,454 feet tall. How many times would you have to stack the Sears Tower on top of itself to reach the moon?

Number and Operations

79

At Millie's Muffins, there is a jellybean mystery jar. If you solve the jellybean mystery, you win a dozen muffins. Here is the information written on the jar:

- There are 1,469 jellybeans in the jar.
- There are 215 more red jellybeans than yellow.
- How many jellybeans are there of each color?

Algebra

80

Ashley and Lindsay spent the afternoon at the mall. They began with $15.00 between them. Lindsay started out with $5.00 more than Ashley, but spent twice as much as Ashley. If, at the end of the day, Lindsay has $2.00 left and Ashley has money left as well, how much did Ashley spend?

Probability

Use two regular six-sided dice.

If you roll both dice 20 times, how often do you think you will roll two even numbers together? Make a prediction. Then try it. Roll the dice 20 times. Record the numbers you roll each time. Compare your results with your prediction. Are they close?

Logical Reasoning

Boris works at the Holiday Shop. He is currently stocking Halloween candy. He puts orange, black, and white candies in boxes. After he fills a box, $\frac{1}{3}$ is orange, $\frac{1}{6}$ is black, and 24 are white. How many candies does Boris put in each box? How many of each color? If necessary, use a diagram to solve this problem.

Number and Operations

What are the mystery numbers?

We are twin primes, or a pair of numbers that have a difference of two.

We are greater than 100 and less than 200.

The sum of the digits of the first number times the sum of the digits of the second number is 80.

What numbers are we?

Patterns and Functions

Abby and Louis are trying to break the school record for jumping on a trampoline. The sixth graders take turns jumping for an hour. Louis consistently makes 10% fewer jumps than Abby. Abby increases the number of jumps she makes in an hour by 20 each hour she jumps. During her first hour, she jumped 200 times. Based on this, how many jumps did Louis make during his fifth hour on the trampoline?

Measurement

The average American consumes 3,642 calories daily. Just being alive burns about 100 calories per hour. If a person does no exercise for a year, how many unburned calories will he or she have at the end of the year? By how many calories could this person afford to reduce his or her diet without eating too few calories?

Geometry

Use one set of tangram pieces.

Using just four tangram pieces, can you form a figure with two acute angles? Can you form a figure with no more than three right angles?

Problem Solving

87

Music 'n' More is having a sale. If you buy five tapes or CDs, you receive a 10% discount on the total price. Each additional tape or CD adds another $\frac{1}{2}$ % discount.

a How many tapes or CDs would you have to buy to receive a 15% discount on your total price?

b What would happen if you purchased 100 CDs?

c Would Music 'n' More want to repeat this sale?

Number and Operations

88

Which of the following numbers has exactly five factors?

16   30   32   33

Measurement

Tanya and Logan have agreed to wash all of the windows on the Flanahan's greenhouse over the next few weeks. The greenhouse has 4,000 panes of 1 foot x 3 feet glass. Mr. Flanahan offered to pay 10¢ a square foot. Logan said he would rather get 30¢ a pane. Which way is the best deal for Tanya and Logan?

Logical Reasoning

Jillanne is at the petting zoo with her little sister. There are 29 rabbits and goats at the zoo. There are 21 goats and lambs, and 32 lambs and rabbits. How many of each kind of animal are at the petting zoo?

Patterns and Functions

Arrange the digits below in given patterns to find the highest or lowest possible answer.

$$\begin{array}{r}\square\square\square \\ -\ \square\square\square \\ \hline \end{array}$$ Digits 1–6
Highest possible difference

$$\begin{array}{r}\square\square\square \\ \times\quad\ \square\square \\ \hline \end{array}$$ Digits 1–5
Lowest possible product

Number and Operations

Alan has 95 cents. He has more quarters than dimes and more nickels than dimes. What coins could he have?

Probability

Sue and Drew each have a deck of 52 cards. Each randomly selects one card. What are the chances of both Sue and Drew drawing a king? Explain how you came up with that answer.

Problem Solving

Franz's Fruits is having an unusual sale. He is allowing other fruit retailers to come in and "buy" his fruit with their own. Here are Franz's prices.

> 4 mangoes = 3 kumquats
> 3 persimmons = 2 bananas
> 7 gooseberries = 1 lime
> 2 apples = 1 mango
> 1 persimmon = 1 apple
> 14 gooseberries = 1 banana

a Sid comes in to "spend" 15 kumquats. How many mangoes can he buy?

b Suppose Sid wants to buy an equal number of apples and persimmons with his 15 kumquats. How many of each can he buy?

Measurement

For each problem, circle the measurement that best fits.

1 Normal body temperature   a. 37° C   b. 67° C   c. 47° C

2 Refrigerator temperature   a. -4° C   b. 4° C   c. 14° C

3 Weight of an average man   a. 790 kg   b. 79 kg   c. 7,900 g

4 Weight of an average dog   a. 18 g   b. 18 kg   c. 180 kg

Geometry

This shape has been folded into a cube.

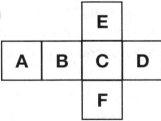

Here are different views of the same cube. For each view, write which letter is on the bottom of the cube.

Logical Reasoning

Brett collects Ping-Pong balls. Isabel collects postage stamps. Brett thinks three balls are as valuable as two stamps. If Isabel agrees to swap 14 stamps, how many balls will Brett need to give her?

Number and Operations

After the holidays, everything at Rollen's Department Store is discounted. From 9 A.M. to 9 P.M. nothing is full price. Calculate the discounts and subtract from the regular prices. Write the pre-tax prices on the sale tags.

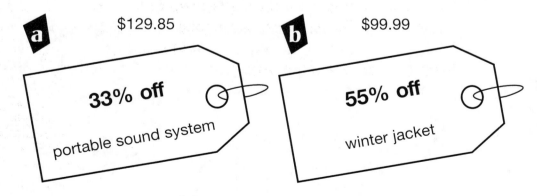

a $129.85
33% off
portable sound system

b $99.99
55% off
winter jacket

Measurement

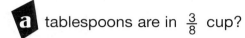

99

There are 3 teaspoons in every tablespoon and 16 tablespoons in every cup. Can you tell how many

a tablespoons are in $\frac{3}{8}$ cup?

b teaspoons are in 2 cups?

c tablespoons are in one gallon?

Algebra

100

Flimzon sold three small spacecraft to Alien Spacelines. Flimzon's prices were unusual. He charged extra for the radio, the heating system, and the seats. The radio cost three times as much as the heating system, and the heating system cost $\frac{1}{5}$ the price of the seats. The seats were 10% of the total selling price of $2,346,236.00. What was the cost of the radio, the heating system, and the seats?

Problem Solving

The problems below each use a different code. Decide which letter represents which number from 0 to 9 to yield a correct sum or difference. Remember these rules:

1. No two letters may have the same number assigned to them.
2. Within a problem, a letter always represents the same digit.
3. The left-hand digit may not be zero.

Find two solutions to each of these problems.

```
    N I N E
 –  F I V E
 ─────────
    F O U R
```

```
    R A I N
 +  S U N
 ─────────
  F O O D
```

Probability

Find the chances of drawing a certain amount of money from the coins below. Assume that coins are always drawn at random and that coins are not replaced. Reduce fractions to lowest terms.

a The chance of getting 50¢ in two draws is _____.

b The chance of getting 26¢ in two draws is _____.

0-7424-1796-4 *Daily Warmups*

Patterns and Functions

Helen is having trouble with her addition. She has just completed these four problems. Her teacher is completely bewildered. Can you find a pattern in Helen's work? She is really making just one simple mistake.

```
   54        906        853        43
 + 62      + 231      + 672      + 81
 ----      -----      -----      ----
   17        147        436        25
```

What is the pattern?

Measurement

Each scrambled word is a unit of measurement. On the first blank, write each measurement spelled correctly. On the second blank, tell what each measures (length, time, distance, etc.).

a T R I M E L O K E _____ _____

b L A L O N G _____ _____

c C L I B E E D _____ _____

d S L U B E H _____ _____

Geometry

Draw a square with corners A, B, C, and D so that side AD is parallel to side BC and side AB is parallel to side DC.

Number and Operations

Overdue books at the Fairfield Library are very much frowned upon. To discourage the late return of materials, each day this library charges a fine of 70¢ per book and 65¢ per magazine. Emma is returning 3 books that are a week late and 5 magazines that are two weeks late. How much is her total fine?

Logical Reasoning

Josh and Miriam are brother and sister. They do not have any other siblings. Both are married and have children. Carolyn is Josh's wife. Austin and Ryan are cousins. Ryan is not Josh's son. Who is Austin's mother?

Algebra

Use centimeter cubes.

Nina ran an errand for her mom. She went to the store and bought 24 pieces of fruit. She purchased three times as many oranges as bananas. On her way home, she dropped twice as many oranges as bananas but still managed to deliver more than a dozen pieces of fruit to her mom. What did she deliver?

Problem Solving

Tracy leaves from home at 10:30 A.M. and drives for 45 minutes. She has a one-hour appointment at the doctor and then drives 45 minutes to get back home. What time is it when she returns home?

Patterns and Functions

Maggie sells magazines. She always places eight on a shelf. She looks at the total number of pages in each issue as she places them in her newsstand. These are the number of pages of each magazine currently on each shelf.

Shelf 1: 110, 38, 69, 77, 83, 52, 38, 53
Shelf 2: 75, 64, 80, 95, 58, 103, 49, 56
Shelf 3: 49, 65, 93, 86, 72, 54, 21, 40

A customer purchased a magazine from shelf 3 containing 54 pages. Maggie did not have an identical issue, so she replaced it with one with 74 pages. What is Maggie's pattern?

Statistics

After their trip to the amusement park, Mr. Michael's class collected the following data. Use the data from the table to find the range, mean, median, and mode.

Students on buses

Bus #	# of students
243	75
211	73
165	74
189	73
239	72

range: _____   median: _____

mean: _____   mode: _____

Number and Operations

Use digits to write twenty-five million, twenty thousand, two hundred fifty, and twenty-five thousandths.

Measurement

Cindy works in a candy store. She puts 12 ounces of nuts in a gift box and then adds 14 ounces of mints and 22 ounces of chocolates. Next she adds 10 ounces of taffy but removes 4 ounces of mints. How many pounds of treats are in the box?

Geometry

Draw parallelogram PQRS. Make segment $\overline{PQ}$ parallel to segment $\overline{RS}$. Make $\overline{PQ}$ and $\overline{RS}$ horizontal segments. Make segments $\overline{PS}$ and $\overline{QR}$ shorter than the horizontal segments.

Algebra

Matt and Will decided to start a handyman's service. They planned to work on six projects over the long weekend. They estimated that each job would take a certain amount of time. To their surprise, each job took three times that long. If the total time spend on the projects was 36 hours, and if each job took the same amount of time, what was their estimate of how long each job would take?

Problem Solving

Ms. Flynn's sixth-grade class won a trip to a nearby amusement park. Tito is waiting to ride the Cliff Drop, which can accommodate 720 people each hour. He has 444 people in front of him. How long until he gets to ride? Taisha is in line for the Plunger. A sign announces a 15-minute wait. There are 330 people in front of Taisha. How many people per minute does this ride accommodate?

Patterns and Functions

What do the numbers in each set have in common?

 a 1, 4, 12, 3, 16, 6, 8

 b 31, 17, 5, 23, 19

Logical Reasoning

Arrange the numbers from 5 to 13 in the circles so that the sum of each row, column, and diagonal is 27.

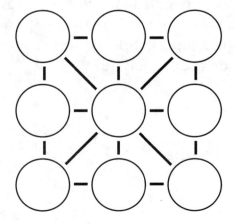

Probability

The Glee Club has designed five school-spirit flags that can be waved during sporting and other school events. How many different ways can the flags be arranged along the sidelines?

Geometry

How much space do you need to play?

A regulation basketball floor is 94 feet by 50 feet.

A regulation baseball diamond is 90 feet on a side.

A regulation volleyball court is 30 yards by 15 yards.

Which sport requires the greatest area?

Number and Operations

Which set of numbers has the greatest common factor?

 a 42, 56, 84

 b 34, 85, 102

 c 39, 78, 130

Measurement

 a It was 5° C outside at noon. Two hours later, the temperature had dropped 8 degrees. What was the temperature outside at 2:00?

 b At 3:00, it was ⁻6° F. The wind chill made it feel like ⁻10° F. How much colder did the wind chill make the temperature seem?

Problem Solving

 123

Read the clues to find the mystery number.

 Clue 1 I am an even factor of 40.

 Clue 2 I am divisible by the only odd factor of 40 that is not 1.

Clue 3 When I am divided by 7, I have a remainder of 5.

What number am I?

Probability

 124

Look at the data. Then answer the questions.

Hair	Suit
purple	polka dots
red	large stripes
blue	swirls
green	solid
orange	

 a How many possible combinations does Yancy have for a clown costume?

 b What is the probability that Yancy will have red hair and a suit with large stripes?

Algebra

Jennie's assignment was to poll 100 classmates to learn what they wanted to be when they grew up. Jennie polled her classmates, grouped the responses, and made the following information chart. Design a pie graph to display her data.

Category	# of Students
business	20
health	15
science	10
education	5
government	5
entertainment	30
other	15

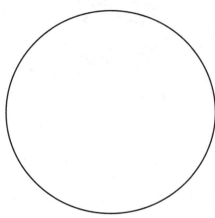

Patterns and Functions

Look for a pattern in these number pairs: 1, 31; 2, 28; 3, 31; 4, 30.

 What number would follow 5?

 What number would follow 9?

Logical Reasoning

Kelsey and Kevin each have the same amount of money in their piggy banks. How much money would Kevin have to give Kelsey so that she had $5.00 more than he had?

Problem Solving

The value of a coin is determined by its age, rarity, and condition. An 1851 large cent costs $23.50. In uncirculated condition, it costs $195.

a What is the cost difference?

b What is the percentage difference?

Geometry

Quinn is planning a garden for next spring. He wants to choose from one of the plots below. Before he decides, he needs to know the area and perimeter of each plot to determine the number of plants he needs and the amount of edging or fencing needed. Help him calculate the perimeter and area of each plot.

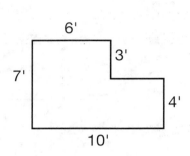

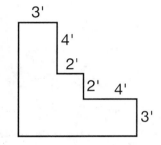

area: _____   area: _____

perimeter: _____   perimeter: _____

Measurement

Meg wants to buy 2.36 kilograms of seed. The seed comes in 20-gram packages. How many packages does she need to buy?

Algebra

Simon built a car that operates on melting ice. The car holds one 50-pound block of ice. The ice melts at a rate of 2 pounds per hour for every 10 degrees of temperature. How long will the ice last at the temperatures shown in the table?

Temperature	Pounds Melted Per Hour	Time Ice Lasts
70°	14	3 hours 34 mins.
75°		
80°		
85°		
90°		

Number and Operations

If Craig maintains a balance of $1,250 for one year on his credit card and is charged 18% simple interest, how much will he have to pay in interest?

Probability

Emilio and Clarissa are playing a board game. A player must roll a 1 or a 6 in order to move a playing piece (or "man") out onto the board. Emilio rolls a 1 and starts his first man. Clarissa rolls a 3. On his next turn, Emilio rolls a 6 and starts another man. Clarissa rolls a 5. On the next turn, what is the probability that . . .

 Emilio will be able to start a third man?

 Clarissa will be able to start her first man?

Logical Reasoning

Four old friends, Jerry, Gene, Jen, and Jules, gather at a high school reunion. They are surprised to learn that all four have chosen unusual professions. One is an animal trainer, one is a butterfly breeder, the third is a professional hockey player, and the fourth is an underwater explorer. Jules is the only one in the group who swims. Jen does not like insects, and Gene does not work with animals. Either Gene or Jules is the goalie, and either Jerry or Jen is the animal trainer. Who has what job?

Patterns and Functions

Arrange each pattern of numbers to equal 100. You may change the order, use any of the four operations, and include parentheses and brackets if necessary.

 20, 30, 40, 50

 5, 10, 15, 20, 25

Measurement

Give the approximate temperature in both Fahrenheit and Celsius for:

a the freezing point of water

b the boiling point of water

c room temperature

d body temperature

Geometry

Toby is excited about walking through the first big snowfall of the winter. He puts on his boots and marches out the back door. He walks 8 feet to the north, then 4 feet to the east, 4 feet south, then 4 feet east, 4 feet north, then 4 feet east, 8 feet south, and 12 feet west to end up back where he started. What is the perimeter of the shape Toby just made? Hint: Make a drawing and label the dimensions.

Algebra

A cat weighs 10 pounds plus half its weight. Write an equation that will help you find the cat's weight, and then solve it.

Patterns and Functions

Dr. Whosit has created an amazing motor which runs on rubbish, the more the better. With just $\frac{3}{4}$ of a pound of rubbish in the converter chamber, the motor produces 10 horsepower. Each additional pound of rubbish increases the production of the motor by 2.5 horsepower. List the horsepower produced by the following weights of trash:

3.75 pounds: _____
5.75 pounds: _____
7.75 pounds: _____

Continue this pattern to determine how many pounds of rubbish are needed to generate 50 horsepower.

Number and Operations

Which of these numbers are divisible by 3? Do you know a rule that will help you with this problem?

a 72   **b** 513   **c** 6,711   **d** 71,350   **e** 84,001

Measurement

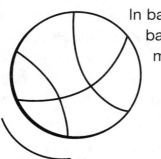

In basketball, the free throw line is 15 feet from the basket. If Lisa shoots 6 free throws in a game, how many inches does she shoot?

Problem Solving

Mr. Prosch's gross weekly salary is $689.00. He has the following deductions withheld from his check: 15% federal income tax, 7.2% social security, and 5% state tax. What is his take-home pay? Mrs. Prosch's annual salary is $32,870.00. What is her gross weekly pay, to the nearest dollar?

0-7424-1796-4 *Daily Warmups*

Statistics

Pick a sentence that you wrote sometime during the day. Create a frequency chart that shows how often each letter of the alphabet was used in your sentence. Then compare your frequency chart with one that your classmates made. Which letters appear most frequently? Which appear least frequently?

Patterns and Functions

Use pattern blocks.

Build each triangle shown. Then build the next three larger triangles. Record how many blocks you used to build each triangle. Then write a rule that would tell someone how many blocks there would be in the tenth triangle.

 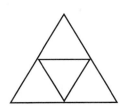 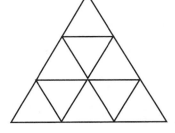

Geometry

Draw a diagram of 4 intersecting circles that form 9 regions. Draw a second set of 4 circles that form 11 regions.

Number and Operations

The five members of the Linguini family love to play darts. At a recent family tournament, they scored a total of 350 points. Each person's score falls between 1 and 100. Each score is evenly divisible by 10. What are the five scores?

Logical Reasoning

Place each of the numerals 1, 2, 3, 4, and 5 in the circles of the
T so that the sum of the three numbers in each direction is the same.
Try to find several different ways to do this.

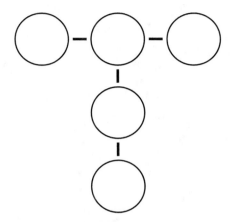

Measurement

Light travels 186,000 miles per second. How many miles would it
travel in an hour? The sun is about 93,000,000 miles from the earth.
About how long does it take for light from the sun to reach the earth?

Number and Operations

Rewrite these fractions so that they share the lowest common denominator:

$$\frac{5}{18} \qquad \frac{7}{30} \qquad \frac{11}{54}$$

Problem Solving

The Environmental Protection Agency stated that each person in the United States generates 3.5 pounds of garbage a day. How many pounds is that for a population of 250,000,000? If 33% of the garbage were recycled, how many pounds would that be?

Algebra

Arrange the integers -5, -4, -3, -2, -1, 0, 1, 2, 3 (using each only once) so that the sum of each row, column, and diagonal is the same. What is the magic sum?

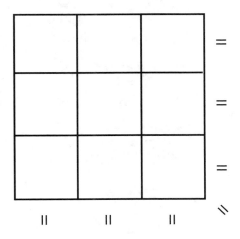

Logical Reasoning

In the town of Buggsville, the residents hold an annual event that includes an unusual race. In this race, groups of people dress up as centipedes and spiders and run together. Centipedes need seven people, and spiders need four people. In this year's race, there were 105 centipedes and spiders for a total of 1,230 racing legs. How many people were dressed as centipedes and how many were dressed as spiders?

153

Measurement

Ben, Bill, and Bob ran a race. Ben ran 880 yards, Bill ran 805 meters, and Bob ran 2,640 feet. Who ran the greatest distance?

154

Geometry

Find the area of each shaded part.

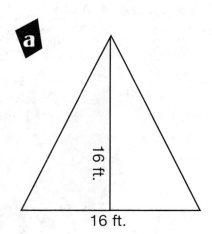

a

16 ft.

16 ft.

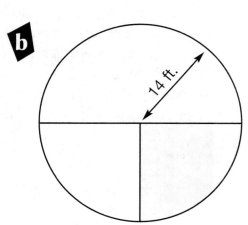

b

14 ft.

Problem Solving

In 1841, 20 wagons and 69 pioneers traveled the Oregon Trail.
In 1850, Army officers counted 44,527 people and 9,927 wagons.
About how many times more people passed in 1850 than in 1841?
About how many times more wagons passed in 1850 than in 1841?

Patterns and Functions

Each day, Peter's little brother Eric gets an allowance. This is Eric's allowance schedule: On the first Monday of the month, he is given 1¢. Then his father doubles his allowance each day for the rest of the week. On the second Monday of the month, he is given 2¢, and the amount doubles each day for six days. On the third Monday, he is given 3¢ and the amount doubles every day for six days. On the fourth Monday, he is given 4¢ and the amount doubles each day for six days. Peter, on the other hand, gets an allowance of $2.50 each week. Which brother receives more allowance money by the end of four weeks? By how much?

Number and Operations

Find the sum of twenty-one million, forty-eight thousand, six hundred seven plus nine million, nine hundred one thousand, four hundred thirteen. Write your answer in word form.

Statistics

This graph shows the sad state of Andrew's savings account, which now has a zero balance. Use the pie graph to determine the ratio of money he spent on tickets for concerts and other entertainment to the money he spent for subscriptions to his favorite magazines. Then figure out the ratio of dollars spent on refreshments to dollars spent for tickets. What percentage of his money did he lose?

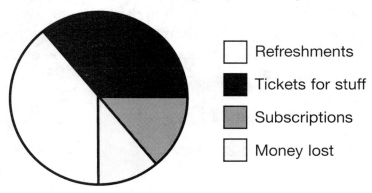

Refreshments

Tickets for stuff

Subscriptions

Money lost

Measurement

Salina went to the grocery store and ordered a pound of bacon. The butcher told her, "We don't sell bacon by the pound. We sell it by the gram." If a kilogram of bacon is 2.2 pounds, how many grams would this be?

Problem Solving

Isabel and Eliza are working on the crime prevention campaign. They are painting reflective address numbers on the curbs in front of the houses in their neighborhood. Over the weekend, the two girls painted a total of 2,000 digits. Each address is made up of four digits. How many complete address numbers did each girl paint if Eliza painted 50% more addresses than Isabel?

Algebra

The sum of the numbers along each side of this hexagon is the same number. Complete the hexagon. What is the magic sum?

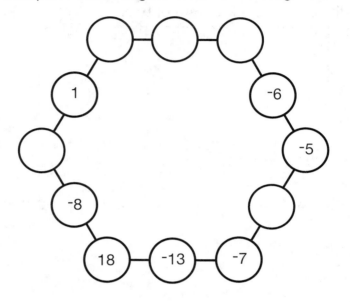

Logical Reasoning

The Student Council arranged chairs on the gymnasium floor for a special program. Rachel sat in a chair in a row with 7 chairs on each side of her. The row she sat in was fifth from the front and sixth from the rear. How many people can be seated in the gymnasium in all?

Geometry

Find the area of each unshaded part.

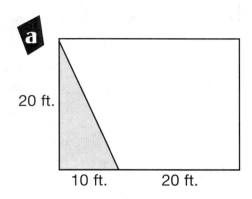

20 ft.

10 ft.   20 ft.

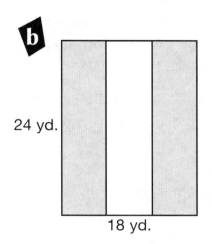

24 yd.

18 yd.

Number and Operations

Which set correctly lists the prime factors of 4,290?

 a 3 x 10 x 11 x 13

 b 2 x 3 x 7 x 11 x 11

 c 2 x 3 x 5 x 11 x 13

 d 2 x 3 x 5 x 143

Measurement

The sixth-grade patio was supposed to be a square with a side length of 50 feet. The Science Club needed one-half of the area for a native plant garden, so the patio was cut in half diagonally. What is the new area of the patio?

Problem Solving

Elena's mantel clock strikes every hour, which is not unusual. However, hers is a 24-hour clock, which means that at 1 P.M., the clock strikes 13 o'clock, or 13 times. In a full 24-hour day, how many times will the clock strike in a full 24-hour day?

Logical Reasoning

Floyd's excavation crew has just been hired to dig out an area for a new office building. The building plans call for a large basement, but Floyd's backhoe is in the repair shop. He needs to hire several workers immediately to dig the basement by hand if he wants to keep the job. Eight of Floyd's employees work all day for 8 days with 8 shovels and remove 8 cubic meters of earth. If he hires 12 new workers with 12 shovels (working at the same rate) to remove the remaining 12 cubic meters of earth, how long should Floyd expect the job to take?

Statistics

Mrs. Lee holds a Field Day for her students every year that includes lots of silly events. This year Antoine, Fritz, Tamar, Huong, and Chelsea had to fill a bathtub in five minutes using only 12-ounce drinking cups. The table below illustrates the number of trips each student made from the barrel of water set up for this contest to the bathtub.

Antoine	Fritz	Tamar	Huong	Chelsea
18	14	16	19	16

Write four questions about the activity for someone in your class to answer.

Geometry

Use graph paper or make a rough sketch of a graph. Number the horizontal axis from 0 to 4. Number the vertical axis from 0 to 8 (or more). Plot the group of points described by these ordered pairs. Connect the points in the order drawn, and connect the last point with the first point. What shape have you made? (0,2) (0,6) (4,8) (4,4)

Algebra

Solve the problem using the formula given.

Snigley is 90 miles from Scottstown. How long would it take Taylor to drive round trip at 60 mph? ($d = rt$)

Number and Operations

171

Use the digits 4–9 one time each to write an equation. Form only whole numbers and use each digit exactly once in each equation. Write an equation with:

a the highest possible sum

b the smallest possible sum

c the largest possible product

Measurement

172

If you multiply the number of yards in a certain distance by 36, you will get the equivalent distance in inches. If you multiply pounds by 16, you will get the equivalent weight in ounces. Use this method to answer the following.

a Multiply days by 86,400 to find _____.

b Multiply cubic yards by 27 to find _____.

c Multiply miles per hour by 88 to find _____.

Patterns and Functions

Cora invented her very own brand of "trick" math. Here are some of her problems:

17 + 25 = 312   9 + 64 = 613   48 + 21 = 69

Find the trick to Cora's math, and then give her answer to 37 + 54.

Geometry

The Parents' Group is planning to build a single pizza for the entire school body. If the radius of the pizza will be four feet, what will be the area?

Number and Operations

Disposable diapers make up 2% of landfill waste. If there are 6,000 landfills, how many of them would disposable diapers fill?

Problem Solving

The circumference of the earth is about 25,000 miles. The space shuttle Discovery went around the earth 64 times. How many miles did it travel?

Statistics

This graph shows the individual heights of the 20 clowns who work for the Party Clowns Service.

What does the information show you about the clowns who work for the service? List at least three facts.

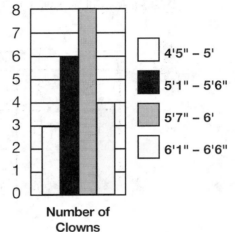

Number of Clowns

Legend:
- ☐ 4'5" – 5'
- ■ 5'1" – 5'6"
- ▨ 5'7" – 6'
- ☐ 6'1" – 6'6"

1.

2.

3.

Number and Operations

What is the lowest number that is divisible by 3, 4, and 5? What is the largest number under 500 that is divisible by 3, 4, and 5?

Algebra

Complete the following by adding across and subtracting down.
The circled number is both a sum and a difference.

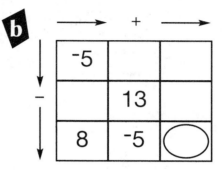

Measurement

What units of measurement are used in each line below? Each
initial stands for a word. For example, 7 D. in a W. = 7 days in a week.

a 4 P. in a B.

b 100 C. in a M.

c 12 E. in a D.

d 1000 Y. in a M.

Geometry

Use what you know about triangles to solve this problem.

A ten-foot ladder is leaning against the side of a house as shown in the drawing. How far up the house does the ladder reach?

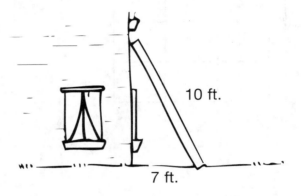

10 ft.

7 ft.

Logical Reasoning

Here is a logical arrangement of the numerals 0 to 9. What is the pattern or rule?

8   5   4   9   1   7   6   3   2   0

Problem Solving

The following problems use every digit 1–9 exactly once when completed properly. Guess which number is the missing factor in each, and then check your guesses using your calculator. Write down the completed problem and answer when you find a solution that uses all nine digits.

 a 1,963 x ___ = ___ ___ ___ ___   **b** 1,738 x ___ = ___ ___ ___ ___

c 159 x ___ ___ = ___ ___ ___ ___   **d** 198 x ___ ___ = ___ ___ ___ ___

Number and Operations

The number 4 is a square number because 2 x 2 = 4. The number 25 is a square number because 5 x 5 = 25. Which of these are square numbers?

64   75   81   131   196   256   300

Measurement

Multiply the number of months in a year by the number of inches in a yard. Add the number of feet in a mile. Divide this by the number of ounces in a pound. Subtract the number of minutes in an hour. Divide by the number of feet in a yard. Add the number of days in a leap year. Add the number of donuts in three dozen. What's your final answer?

Probability

Make a spinner like the one shown here. Put a pencil in the center, holding a paper clip. Spin the paper clip.

Before spinning, predict where the pointer will stop. Write your prediction in column 1. In column 2, write the probability that you will be correct. Then spin until your prediction comes true. In column 3, record the number of times you had to spin before your prediction became true. Try this two or three times. Are you good at guessing the correct spot?

Prediction	Probability	Spins Needed

Number and Operations

187

The flesh-eating dinosaur Tyrannosaurus Rex had a large mouth filled with 6-inch teeth. The largest human tooth (canine) is about $\frac{3}{8}$ of an inch long. How many human teeth would it take to make one Tyrannosaurus tooth?

Logical Reasoning

188

A famous manuscript is on display in a museum case. To what pages is the manuscript open if the product of the page numbers is 9,312?

Algebra

For each problem, find two numbers whose product is the top number and whose sum is the bottom number.

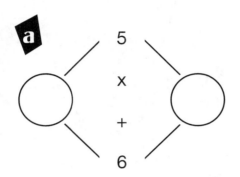

a 5

x

+

6

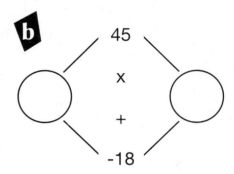

b 45

x

+

-18

Number and Operations

Kara is writing a sports article for the school newsletter. She wants to compare the girls' basketball team's win-loss ratio to the boys' basketball team's win-loss ratio. The boys' team has won 12 of their 15 games. The girls' team has won 16 of their 20 games. Find the win-loss ratio for each team.

Geometry

Use the clues given to draw a picture of the shape described.
Write the name of each shape.

a I have six sides.
All of my sides are the same length.
Every side has a side to which it is parallel.
What am I? _____

b I have three sides.
All three sides are the same length.
None of the sides are perpendicular or parallel.
What am I? _____

Measurement

Ruth dribbles the ball the entire length of the basketball court
(94 feet) and scores a basket. How many inches does the ball travel
across the court?

Probability

If you roll two dice, is there a greater chance of rolling a pair or of rolling a sum of 10?

Problem Solving

Allyson, Bob, Chad, Danielle, and Emily sit in the same row of desks in math class. The two boys sit one after the other. Danielle, the tallest, sits in the last seat. Chad sits right in front of his twin sister. Allyson sits in between the other two girls. In which order are the five students sitting? Hint: Draw a picture to help you solve this problem.

0-7424-1796-4 *Daily Warmups*

Algebra

Brussels sprouts come in 3-pound and 5-pound bags, which cost $1.15 and $1.63 respectively. How many of each should the school cafeteria buy in order to have at least 17 pounds of Brussels sprouts at the lowest cost?

Number and Operations

It takes our solar system over 200 years to make one revolution around the center of the Milky Way. If the earth is 4 billion years old, how many revolutions has our solar system made?

Patterns and Functions

Use an 11 x 11-pin geoboard and rubber bands.

Make a square touching eight pins. Now, make another square touching eight pins, but let no more than two of those pins be touched by the first rectangle. How many times can you repeat this pattern?

Measurement

Mira is learning nautical terms. She learns that a fathom is 6 feet and that a league is equal to 3 miles. Help her to answer the question: Which is longer—25,000 fathoms or 30 leagues?

Geometry

Use graph paper or make a rough sketch of a graph. Draw all four quadrants, using positive numbers up to 6 and negative numbers through ⁻6. Plot the group of points described by these ordered pairs. Connect the points in the order drawn, and connect the last point with the first point. What shape have you drawn?

(3, ⁻3) (6, 2) (⁻6, 2) (⁻3, ⁻3)

Probability

You may want to use centimeter cubes to work out this problem.

Josie and her friends each have three tickets to use at the fair. They have these options for activities. They could go through a haunted house, ride the roller coaster, ride bumper cars, watch a clown act, or attend a mini-concert. How many different combinations of three activities are possible if they do not choose the same activity twice? List some of them.

Published by Instructional Fair. Copyright protected.

0-7424-1796-4 *Daily Warmups*

Problem Solving

Duke, Cindy's Great Dane, ate 125 hot dogs over a five-day period. Each day, he ate seven more hot dogs than on the previous day. How many hot dogs did he eat on the first day? Hint: Make a chart.

Number and Operations

Use the following numbers to make the four equations below each equal 24.

-8, -6, -4, 3, 8, 8, 16, 32

____ x ____ = 24

____ x ____ = 24

____ + ____ = 24

____ + ____ = 24

0-7424-1796-4 *Daily Warmups*

Algebra

As Roselle looked through her binoculars at five cardinals, she also spotted six blue jays. The next day she saw 10 cardinals and 10 blue jays. On the third day she spied 15 cardinals and 14 blue jays. On the fourth day she spotted 20 cardinals and 18 blue jays. If this pattern continues, on what day will Roselle see 10 more cardinals than blue jays? You may wish to make a table like this to help you solve the problem:

Day	1	2	3	
Cardinals	5			
Blue Jays	6			

Number and Operations

Look at the box below. Only one of the numbers is not a square of another number. Which number is it?

7	4,096	64	196
121	13	81	12
14	2,401	6,561	9
11	8	49	144

0-7424-1796-4 *Daily Warmups*

Geometry

Is each statement true of a rectangle, a square, a parallelogram, or a combination of these shapes?

a This shape has four right angles.

b This shape has pairs of parallel opposite sides of the same lengths.

c This shape must have all sides the same length.

d This shape may or may not have right angles.

Patterns and Functions

The Halls are moving across town. Four of Cameron's friends—Sean, Beau, Lloyd, and Emilio—have agreed to help Cameron load his furniture onto the truck. The four friends form a line from the truck to Cameron's room and begin passing furniture from one person to another. How many different ways can the boys line up?

Number and Operations

A car dealer offers an immediate cash rebate of $1,000, an equipment discount of $400, and a deal for a cellular telephone that lists for $400 for $100. If a buyer purchases the car and the telephone for a total of $15,900, what was the original price of the car?

Logical Reasoning

Begin with the number 1,234. Rearrange two adjacent numbers at a time. What is the fewest number of steps it will take before you can write the number 4,321?

Problem Solving

In how many different ways can a panel of five on-off switches be set if no two adjacent switches can be off?

Measurement

If you multiply inches by 2.54, you will convert that distance to centimeters. Use this method to complete each of these statements.

a Multiply inches by 25.4 to find _____.

b Subtract 32 from °F and divide by 1.8 to find _____.

c Multiply British Thermal Units (BTUs) by 0.0002928 to find _____.

Number and Operations

A deficient number is one in which the sum of the factors, not including the number itself, is less than the number. For example, 4 is a deficient number because the factors of 4 are 1 and 2, which have a sum of 3. Which of the following are deficient numbers?

21   23   30   50

Geometry

What geometrical terms can be spelled with each set of letters? Unscramble each word and then draw the shape.

 cootgan   shmobru   gacnode

Patterns and Functions

Give the number that comes next in each progression.

a 5, 3, 7, 4, 8

b 10, 5, 20, 10, 40

c 9, 6, 12, 13, 10, 20

d 100, 91, 84, 79, 76

Probability

The odds of finding a cracked egg in a shipment of eggs are 1 egg in 24 cartons before those cartons are placed on grocery store shelves. Once they are on shelves, however, your odds of getting a cracked egg rise to 1 egg in every 10 cartons. Each carton holds a dozen eggs. How many cracked eggs can a grocer expect to find in a shipment of 2,880 eggs just off the truck? How many more of these eggs will be cracked after being placed on shelves? About what percent of the total shipment of eggs will be broken?

Number and Operations

Read the clues to find the mystery number.

 This number is a factor of 84 but not of 96.

 When the number is doubled and then divided by 6, the remainder is 2.

 The number is greater than 10.

What is the mystery number?

Logical Reasoning

If 5 blems are worth 3 frins, and 2 frins are worth 1 scir, then how many scirs are 20 blems worth?

Geometry

After the first snowfall of the season, Marylou runs outside to play. She goes outside and makes a stair-step shape. She walks 20 feet to the south, then 8 feet west, a short distance north, then 11 feet west, another distance to the north, 15 feet west, and another distance to the north. Then she makes a right turn and walks in a straight path directly back to her starting point. What is the perimeter of the shape in yards that Marylou has just made in the snow? Hint: Make a drawing and label the dimensions given. Then find the missing lengths.

Measurement

A section of land is 640 acres. How much is a quarter section?

There are 160 square rods in an acre. How many square rods are there in a 640-acre section of land?

Problem Solving

Stuart has 12 coins in his pocket worth exactly $1.00. He could
have nickels, dimes, and/or quarters. What combinations of coins
could he have? Find all the possibilities.

Probability

If Curt randomly connects two **different** numbers on the face of
a clock and then multiplies them, what are the chances of his
obtaining a product over 100?

Number and Operations

In the presidential election of 1860, Abraham Lincoln received 180 electoral votes. His three opponents received 123 votes. What percentage of electoral votes did Lincoln receive?

Logical Reasoning

Katherine has two buckets of dimes totaling $20. The bucket in her left hand contains $3 more than the bucket in her right hand. How many dimes are in each bucket?

Number and Operations

223

Round this number to the nearest hundredth: four hundred twenty-six and seven hundred fifty-nine thousandths. Write in numerals.

Patterns and Functions

224

Leon has invented a type of "trick" math. Here are three of his examples:

$$8 \times 9 = 9 \qquad 144 \div 12 = 3 \qquad 14 + 15 = 11$$

Find the trick to Leon's math, and then give his answer to 64×3.

Problem Solving

Modern hot-air balloons burn propane to stay afloat. The average balloon carries 60 gallons of propane and burns about 9 gallons each hour. If a hot-air balloon catches a good wind, it can travel about 30 miles in an hour. How far can a balloon travel with a good wind and a full load of propane before it has to set down to refill its tanks?

Number and Operations

Begin with the fraction $\frac{1}{2}$. Make a new fraction by doubling the denominator and keeping 1 for the numerator. Do this again, so you have:

$$\frac{1}{2} + \frac{1}{4} + \frac{1}{8} +$$

Continue this pattern with two more fractions. Do you think the sum of these fractions will be greater than or less than 1? Find the answer. What do you think will happen when you repeat this 10 times? 20 times?

Logical Reasoning

A father and daughter share the same day and month of birth. The father is currently between the ages of 45 and 50. Four years ago, the father was exactly three times as old as his daughter was. This year the daughter is not 19. How old is the father this year?

Geometry

Give the name of each shape described. Be as specific as possible.

a I have three sides. All of my lines intersect, and one pair of lines is perpendicular.

b I have six sides, all of which are the same length. Every side has a side to which it is parallel.

c I have four sides. One pair of sides is parallel; the other sides would intersect if they were extended.

Numbers and Operations

Listed below are four of the Presidents of the United States and their ages at the time of their inaugurations. Their ages are written in Roman numerals. Figure out each age.

a George Washington   LVII = _____

b Franklin Pierce   XLVIII = _____

c Theodore Roosevelt   XLII = _____

d Ronald Reagan   LXIX = _____

Problem Solving

Think of how letters are displayed on a telephone keypad. The number 1 has no letters. On the number 2 are the letters A, B, and C. On the number 3 are the letters D, E, and F, and so on. There is no Q or Z on the keypad. Use the letters on the telephone to spell out the names of three U.S. states.

a 996-6464   **b** 837-6668   **c** 463-4262

Measurement

The air temperature is -7° C. The water temperature is 4° C.
How much warmer is the water temperature?

Algebra

Fill in the spaces to complete the magic square.
What is the magic sum?

-16			-10
6		-4	
	2	4	-8
8	-12	-14	

Number and Operations

Shannon owns a children's shoe store. She carries 12 different styles of boys' shoes, each in a choice of 3 colors. Shannon also sells 15 different styles of girls' shoes, each in a choice of 4 colors. For both boys and girls, she carries every size and half-size from 2 to 11. If her complete inventory is made up of one pair of shoes for each option, how many pairs of shoes does Shannon stock?

Problem Solving

If there are 800,000 species of insects and only 0.1% are harmful, what is the number of harmful species?

Answer Key

Page 6

#1: Aaron is 12; Brendan is 16; Cole is 8; and Devin is 4.

#2: 24 x 5 = 120 oz.; 120 oz. ÷ 16 oz./lb. = 7.5 lbs.

Page 7

#3:

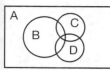

#4: 6,724,582

Page 8

#5: Possible solution: Two right triangles, two squares, or two rectangles.

#6: range: 89; mean: 33.25; median: 18; mode: 18

Page 9

#7: perimeter = 170.71 feet; area = 1,250 square feet

#8: a. 45 pennies, 1 nickel; b. 20 pennies, 1 nickel, 1 quarter; c. 4 nickels, 3 dimes

Page 10

#9: Equation: $.25q + .10d + .05n + .01p = \$0.50$. 32 possible solutions: 2 quarters; 1 quarter, 2 dimes, 1 nickel; 1 quarter, 1 dime, 3 nickels; 1 quarter, 1 dime, 2 nickels, 5 pennies; 1quarter, 1 dime, 1nickel, 10 pennies; 1 quarter, 1 dime, 15 pennies; 5 dimes; 4 dimes, 2 nickels; 4 dimes, 1 nickel, 5 pennies; 4 dimes, 10 pennies; 3 dimes, 4 nickels; 3 dimes, 3 nickels, 5 pennies; and many more.

#10: a parallelogram

Page 11

#11: Set a. is the largest. The GCF for a. is 14, b. is 2, and c. is 7.

#12: 13 minutes, 10 seconds

Page 12

#13: 2,160 feet; $78.12 each

#14: Rachel is 10 and is the firstborn twin.

Page 13

#15: b., d., and e. are divisible by 9. Carlos knew that if the sum of the digits is divisible by 9, then the number is also.

#16: Rule = the number put in is squared

Number in	Number out
12	144
25	625
30	900
10	100
11	121
13	169
18	324
32	1,024

Page 14

#17: The total perimeter is 132 feet, which equals 44 yards. The area increased by 780 sq. ft. The area has quadrupled, from 260 sq. ft. to 1,040 sq. ft.

#18: a. 1 in 2; b. 1 in 4; c. 1 in 8; d. 1 in 16

Page 15

#19: bump 1: 2,250 lbs.; bump 2: 1,687.5 lbs.; bump 3: 1,265.6; bump 4: 929.2; bump 5: 711.9; bump 6: 533.9; bump 7: 400.4; bump 8: 300.3; bump 9: 225.2; bump 10: 168.9 lbs. left

#20: 72; $n \times (n - 1)$

Page 16

#21: 10 combinations

#22: boys' team = 3:1; girls' team = 7:1

Page 17

#23: 90

#24:

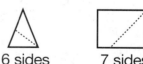

6 sides   7 sides   8 sides

7 sides   8 sides

Page 18

#25: Row 1: Add $\frac{1}{3}$ to each rational number and express in lowest terms.
$\frac{1}{2}, \frac{5}{6}, 1\frac{1}{6}, 1\frac{1}{2}, 1\frac{5}{6}, 2\frac{1}{6}, 2\frac{1}{2}, 2\frac{5}{6}$
Row 2: Multiply each rational number by two.
$\frac{5}{32}, \frac{5}{16}, \frac{5}{8}, 1\frac{1}{4}, 2\frac{1}{2}, 5, 10, 20; 80$

#26: 96 cars; $480.00

Page 19
#27: 1 in 39
#28: Possible answers: 6:00, 12:30, 3:45, 9:15

Page 20
#29: a. 512, 1,024; b. 38, 40; c. 93, 107
#30: a. $\frac{1}{6} + \frac{3}{4} + \frac{1}{12} = 1$
b. $\frac{3}{4} + \frac{1}{4} - \frac{5}{12} = \frac{7}{12}$
c. $\frac{5}{6} + \frac{1}{4} + \frac{1}{3} = 1\frac{5}{12}$
d. $\frac{1}{12} + \frac{5}{6} - \frac{1}{2} = \frac{5}{12}$
e. $\frac{3}{4} + \frac{7}{12} + \frac{1}{2} = 1\frac{5}{6}$

Page 21
#31: Estimates will vary; actual trips = 3,750.
#32: 18 right triangles

Page 22
#33:

1.1	0.4	2.0
1.9	1.5	0.1
0.5	1.6	1.4

#34: seventh hour

Page 23
#35: a. 50, b. 92
#36: 27,120 seconds; answers will vary

Page 24
#37: 16
#38: Joab has a greater chance of getting points: 18 out of 36. Kai's chances are 12 out of 36. The game is unfair.

Page 25
#39: d is impossible.
#40: $9.75

Page 26
#41: youngest, 8; triplets, 12; oldest, 16
#42: $0.68 − 0.55 + 5.57 + 3.98 + 0.99 − 0.50 − 0.25 Total $9.92

Page 27
#43: The pie will be cut similar to the following:
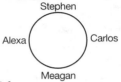
#44: 158 bottles

Page 28
#45: Answers will vary.
#46: Answers will vary. Some possibilities are 505, 353, 151, and 252. Any palindrome with a digit of 5 will work.

Page 29
#47: 36, 0.50, 0.8, 121. Answers may vary; accept any that can be verified.
#48: b., c., d., e., and g. are not regular polygons; the sides and angles on each of those shapes are not equal.

Page 30
#49:
#50: 64

Page 31
#51: the choir, $250.00; the band, $500.00; the student council, $750.00
#52: There is one chance in 1,974. So there is no advantage given the odds.

Page 32
#53: 6 ways
#54: pentagon; triangles are created by diagonals

Page 33
#55: Designs will vary.
#56:

Stephen
Alexa
Carlos
Meagan

Page 34
#57: The batteries will no longer work after charge 6.
#58: Angella, Timothy, Grace, Ramon, Justin

Page 35
#59: 5 times
#60: 105 or 140

Page 36
#61: Answers and shapes may vary. Samples:

6 units   8 units   12 units
#62: Shapes b. and d.

Page 37
#63: 24
#64: 3 + 5 + 7 + 11 + 13 + 17 + 19 + 23

Page 38
#65: 12 people have only sisters; 8 have only brothers.

Brothers (18) 12 6 8 Sisters (14)
#66: 72 sheets of paper

Page 39
#67: 9 offenses, $65.00 fine
#68: greatest number: Friday, 67; fewest number: Thursday, 6; total: 128

Page 40
#69: 2,700 square feet
#70: 28.8 gal, $40.32

Page 41
#71: 21,937,500 gallons
#72: median: 7.5; mode: 6; average: 8.14

Page 42
#73: 6, 7, 8, 9, 10, 11, 12, 13
#74: 7 trips: Take the cat across, leave the cat; cross back; take the bird across, leave bird, pick up cat; cross back; leave cat, pick up rabbit and cross; leave rabbit, cross back; pick up cat, cross river.

Page 43
#75: $4\left(\frac{s}{3}\right) = 24$; $s = 18$
#76: Answers will vary, but with two sets they can make each shape.

triangle   square   pentagon   hexagon

heptagon   octagon

Page 44
#77: Clarissa and Skylar's: 600 ft.; T.J. and Camilla's: 480 ft.
#78: Approximately 867,532 times.

Page 45
#79: red, 842; yellow, 627
#80: $4.00

Page 46
#81: You could expect to roll two even numbers about 5 times in 20. The expected probability is $\frac{9}{36}$, or 25%. Results will vary.
#82: 48 candies in each box: 16 orange, 8 black, 24 white

Page 47
#83: 107 and 109
#84: 252 jumps

Page 48
#85: 453,330 unburned calories. The person could reduce daily intake by 1,242 calories.
#86: Both can be formed; solutions will vary.

Page 49
#87: a. 15. b. 57.5% discount. c. Answers will vary, but there is a point at which you would receive 100% discount.
#88: 16

Page 50
#89: Mr. Flanahan's offer is the best. Under his plan, the kids would be paid 4,000 x 3 sq. ft. x 2 x 0.10 (since there are two sides to a window), equaling $2,400.00. Logan's plan pays them 4,000 x 30¢, or $1,200.00.
#90: 9 goats, 20 rabbits, and 12 lambs

Page 51
#91: a. 654 − 123 = 531
b. 245 x 13 = 3,185
#92: 3 quarters (*q*), 1 dime (*d*), 2 nickels (*n*); 3 q, 4 n; 2 q, 1 d, 7 n; 2 q, 9 n; 1 q, 14 n

Page 52
#93: $\frac{1}{169}$. The chance of either person drawing a king is $\frac{1}{13}$. For both outcomes to occur, we must multiply $\frac{1}{13} \times \frac{1}{13} = \frac{1}{169}$.
#94: a. 20 mangoes; b. 20 apples, 20 persimmons

Page 53
#95: 1. a. 98.6° F; 2. b. 40° F; 3. b. 175 lbs.; 4. b. 40 lbs.
#96: a. F; b. F; c. C

Page 54
#97: 21
#98: a. $87.00; b. $45.00

Page 55
#99: a. 6 T; b. 96 tsp.; c. 256 T
#100: radio: $140,774.16; heating system: $46,924.72; seats: $234,623.60; total: $422,322.48

Page 56
#101: a. 5356 − 2376 = 2980; 3437 − 1457 = 1980;
b. 5831 + 941 = 6772; 2954 + 714 = 3668
#102: a. $\frac{1}{6}$ b. $\frac{2}{4} \times \frac{1}{3} = \frac{1}{6}$

Page 57
#103: Helen is starting to add with the left column and is carrying to the right.
#104: a. kilometer, length; b. gallon, volume; c. decibel, relative loudness; d. bushel, volume

Page 58
#105:

#106: She owes $60.20: $14.70 for books and $45.50 for the magazines.

Page 59
#107: Carolyn
#108: 16 oranges and 5 bananas, 14 oranges and 4 bananas, or 12 oranges and 3 bananas

Page 60
#109: 1:00 P.M.
#110: Maggie always has four even-numbered and four odd-numbered magazines on each shelf. The sum of all the magazines on a shelf is a multiple of 20.

Published by Instructional Fair. Copyright protected.

Page 61
#111: range: 3, median: 73, mean: 73, mode: 73
#112: 25,020,250.025

Page 62
#113: $3\frac{3}{8}$ lbs.
#114: Drawing may vary slightly.

Page 63
#115: 2 hours
#116: 37 minutes; 22 people per minute

Page 64
#117: a. factors of 48; b. prime numbers
#118: Possible solution: 10   5   12
                         11   9   7
                          6 13   8

Page 65
#119: 120
#120: 4,700 sq. ft.; 8,100 sq. ft.; 4,050 sq. ft.; baseball

Page 66
#121: Set b. is the highest with a GCF of 17. Set a. = 14, set c. = 13.
#122: a. -3° C; b. 4° C

Page 67
#123: 40
#124: a. 20; b. 1:20

Page 68
#125:

#126: a. 31; b. 30. Pattern: The first number is the month; the second number is the number of days in that month.

Page 69
#127: $2.50
#128: a. $171.50; b. 88%

Page 70
#129: a. area = 58 sq. ft., perimeter = 34 ft.
        b. area = 49 sq. ft., perimeter = 36 ft.
#130: 118 packages

Page 71
#131: 75: 15 lb., 3 hrs. 20 min.; 80: 16 lb., 3 hrs. 8 min.; 85: 17 lb., 2 hr. 57 min.; 90: 18 lb., 2 hr. 47 min.
#132: $225

Page 72
#133: In both cases, the answer is $\frac{2}{6}$ or $\frac{1}{3}$.
#134: Jerry—butterfly breeder; Gene—professional hockey player; Jen—animal trainer; Jules—underwater explorer

Page 73
#135: a. (50 − 20) + 30 + 40
        b. Answers will vary. One solution:
            [(25 − 15) − 10] + (5 x 20)
#136: a. 32° F, 0° C; b. 212° F, 100° C;
        c. about 72° F, 22° C; d. 98.6° F, 37° C

Page 74
#137: 48 ft.
#138: Let w represent the cat's weight. Then $w = 10 + \frac{1}{2}w$. The cat weighs 20 lb.

Page 75
#139: 17.5 horsepower, 22.5 horsepower, 27.5 horsepower, 16.75 pounds
#140: If the sum of the digits is divisible by 3, then the number is also. Letters a., b., and c. are divisible by 3. The last two are not.

Page 76
#141: 1,080 in.
#142: $501.59, $632.00

Page 77
#143: Answers will vary.
#144: 1, 4, 9, 16, 25, 36. Expressions of the rule may vary. Students may notice that the triangles grow in this way: 1 + 3 + 5 + 7 …and that the series of sums is made up of the square numbers. Students may express the rule as n x n, or n^2, where n is the number of units on the side of the triangle, or the number of the triangle in the series; the tenth triangle will be made of 100 blocks.

Page 78
#145: Possible answers:

#146: 50, 60, 70, 80, 90

Page 79
#147: One possible solution:

#148: 669,600,000 mi., $8\frac{1}{3}$ min.

Page 80
#149: In order: $\frac{75}{270}$, $\frac{63}{270}$, $\frac{55}{270}$
#150: 875,000,000 lbs., 288,750,000 lbs.

Page 81
#151: One possible answer:

2	-5	0
-3	-1	1
-2	3	-4

#152: centipedes: 455 people; spiders: 160 people

Page 82
#153: Bill
#154: a. 64 sq. ft.; b. 153.86 sq. ft.

Page 83
#155: 645 times more people, 496 times more wagons
#156: Eric gets the larger allowance by $2.70.

Page 84
#157: thirty million, nine hundred fifty thousand, twenty
#158: 3:1 = ratio of tickets to subscriptions; 3:3 or 1:1 = ratio of refreshments to tickets; 12.5% = money lost

Page 85
#159: 455 grams
#160: Eliza: 300, Isabel: 200

Page 86
#161:
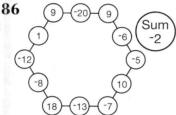
#162: 150. There are 15 chairs in each of 10 rows.

Page 87
#163: a. 500 sq. ft.; b. 144 sq. ft.
#164: set c.

Page 88
#165: 1,250 sq. ft.
#166: 300 times

Page 89
#167: eight days
#168: Answers will vary.

Page 90
#169: a parallelogram
#170: 3 hours

Page 91
#171: a. 98,765 + 4 (98,769); b. One possible solution: 468 + 579 (1,047); c. 964 x 875 (843,500)
#172: a. seconds, b. cubic feet, c. feet per minute (Multiply by 5,280 to find feet per hour, then divide by 60 to find feet per minute.)

Page 92
#173: Cora's answer would be 811. She adds the numbers in the ones' place and writes the number down. She does not carry over any numbers. Then she adds the numbers in the tens' place and writes it down.
#174: 50.24 square feet

Page 93
#175: 120 landfills
#176: 1,600,000 mi.

Page 94
#177: Answers will vary.
#178: 60; 480

Page 95
#179: a.
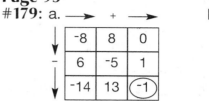
b.
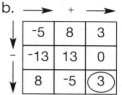
#180: a. pecks in a bushel; b. centimeters in a meter; c. eggs in a dozen; d. years in a millennium

Page 96
#181: $\sqrt{51}$ feet
#182: When written in word form, these numbers appear in alphabetical order.

Page 97
#183: a. 1,963 x 4 = 7,852; b. 1,738 x 4 = 6,952; c. 159 x 48 = 7,632; d. 198 x 27 = 5,346
#184: 64, 81, 196, 256

Page 98
#185: 12 x 36 + 5,280 ÷ 16 − 60 ÷ 3 + 366 + 36 = 501
#186: Results will vary.

Page 99
#187: 16 human teeth
#188: pages 96 and 97

Page 100
#189: a. 1, 5; b. -3, -15
#190: boys' team: 4:1; girls' team: 4:1

Page 101
#191: a. regular hexagon; b. equilateral triangle
#192: 1,128 inches

Page 102
#193: There are six possible pairs but only three ways to reach a sum of 10: 4-6, 5-5, 6-4.
#194: from front to back: Bob, Chad, Emily, Allyson, Danielle

Page 103
#195: one 3-lb. bag and three 5-lb. bags for $6.04
#196: 20,000,000 revolutions

Page 104
#197: Answers will vary.
#198: 30 leagues (475,200 ft.)

Page 105

#199: a trapezoid

#200: 60 possibilities (5 • 4 • 3 = 60); HH, RC, BC; HH, RC, CA; HH, RC, M-C; RC, BC, CA; RC, BC, M-C.

Page 106

#201: He ate 11 hot dogs on the first day.

#202: $^-6 \times {}^-4$; 8×3; $8 + 16$; $32 + {}^-8$

$\frac{4}{66}$ $\frac{2}{33}$

Page 107

#203: Day 12: 60 cardinals and 50 blue jays. $B = 5n$ and $H = 4n + 2$ where n = the number of the day.

#204: 13

Page 108

#205: a. square, rectangle; b. parallelogram, rectangle, square; c. square; d. parallelogram

#206: 24

Page 109

#207: $17,200

#208: 6

Page 110

#209: 13 ways: all on (1 way); 4 on, 1 off (5 ways); 3 on, 2 off (6 ways); 2 on, 3 off (1 way)

#210: a. mm; b. ° C; c. kilowatt-hours

Page 111

#211: 21, 23, 50

#212: a. octagon, b. rhombus, c. decagon

Page 112

#213: a. 4 (− 2, + 4, − 3, + 4, − 4, + 4)
b. 20 (÷ 2, × 4, ÷ 2, × 4)
c. 21 (− 3, × 2, + 1, − 3, × 2, + 1)
d. 75 (− 7, − 5, − 3, − 1)

#214: 10, 14 more, 0.8%

Page 113

#215: 28

#216: 6 scirs (20 blems are four times the 5 blems first mentioned. Four times 3 frins makes 12 frins. Every 2 frins are worth one scir. 6 × 2 = 12)

-16	12	10	-10
6	-6	-4	0
-2	2	4	-8
8	-12	-14	14

Page 114

#217: Total distance = 108 feet, or 36 yards. Missing vertical length = 20; missing horizontal length = 34.

```
        ┌──────────┐
     15 │          │
        └────┐     │ 20
          11 │     │
             └──┐  │
              8 │  │
```

#218: 160 acres; 102,400 sq. rods